GREECE

David Cumming

Photographs by Yiorgos Nikiteas

CHERRYTREE BOOKS

LETTERS FROM AROUND THE WORLD

Titles in this series

**AUSTRALIA • BANGLADESH • BRAZIL • CANADA • CHINA • COSTA RICA
EGYPT • FRANCE • GERMANY • GREECE • INDIA • INDONESIA • ITALY
JAMAICA • JAPAN • KENYA • MEXICO • PAKISTAN • SOUTH AFRICA • SPAIN**

A Cherrytree Book

Conceived and produced by

Nutshell MEDIA
Intergen House
65-67 Western Road
Hove BN3 2JQ, UK
www.nutshellmedialtd.co.uk

Reprinted 2008

First published in 2005 by
Evans Brothers Ltd
2A Portman Mansions
Chiltern Street
London W1U 6NR

VISIT OUR WEBSITE
www.evansbooks.co.uk

© Copyright Evans Brothers 2005

Editor: Polly Goodman
Designer: Mayer Media Ltd
Map artwork: Encompass Graphics Ltd
All other artwork: Mayer Media Ltd

All photographs were taken by Yiorgos Nikiteas.

Acknowledgements
The photographer would like to thank the Stathopoulos family, Plato Rivellis, and the staff and pupils of Agios Yiorgios School, Ermoupolis for all their help with this book.

Printed in China by WKT Co. Ltd

British Library Cataloguing in Publication Data
Cumming, David, 1953–
    Greece. – (Letters from around the world)
    1. Greece – Social conditions – 1974 – Juvenile literature
    2. Greece – Social life and customs – 1974 – Juvenile literature
    I. Title
949.5'076

ISBN 978 1 84234 278 7

Cover: Alkinos (centre, back) with his sister Dafni (centre, front) and friends Yiorgos (right) and his sister Evgenia (left), on the Ermoupolis waterfront.
Title page: Alkinos and his friends climbing a tree.
This page: The ancient Acropolis stands on a hilltop above the capital city, Athens.
Contents page: Alkinos takes aim in a game of handball.
Glossary page: Alkinos playing handball during the morning break at school.
Further Information page: Alkinos learns about the wind and sailing during a geography lesson.
Index: A view across Ermoupolis, the capital of Syros, to uninhabited islands nearby.

Contents

My Country

Thursday, 6 May

P O Box 104
Ano Mana
84-100 Syros
Greece

Dear Nickie,

Yasoo! (You say 'Yah-SOO'. This means 'Hi' in Greek.)

My name is Alkinos Stathopoulos. I'm 11 years old and I live on Syros, an island in Greece. I've got a sister called Dafni, who is 9 years old. Do you have any brothers or sisters?

I'm glad you're learning about Greece at school. I'll try to answer any questions you have about life here.

From

Alkinos

Here I am at home with my dad Yiorgos, mum Sofia and Dafni. ➔

The first great European civilization began in Greece, around 2500 BC. The Ancient Greeks built amazing buildings. They also developed ideas in philosophy and science that are still important today.

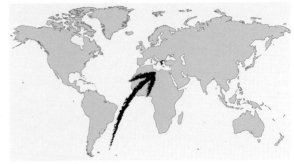

Greece's place in the world.

Greece is in south-east Europe. Many islands surround the Greek mainland.

TURKEY

BULGARIA

MACEDONIA

Thessaloniki

Thracian Sea

Aliákmonas

Limnos

ALBANIA

Olympus (2,917m)

TURKEY

PINDUS MOUNTAINS

Volos

Aegean Sea

Lesbos

Corfu

G R E E C E

IONIAN

Samos

Lefkas

ISLANDS

ATHENS

Andros

Kefalonia

Patrai

Piraeus

Tinos

Mykonos

DODECANESE ISLANDS

Syros

CYCLADES

Kos

N

Zakynthos

Paros

Naxos

Rhodes

Ionian Sea

ISLANDS

0   50   100 kilometres

0   50   100 miles

Sea of Crete

Karpathos

Mediterranean Sea

Crete

5

Syros is one of the Cyclades Islands. It is in the Aegean Sea, between Greece and Turkey. Almost half of the island's population live in Ermoupolis (pronounced 'Air-MO-poliss', the capital and biggest town.

Syros has no water supply of its own. Instead, the salt has to be taken out of seawater so that the water can be used for drinking. The water is piped to all the homes and businesses on the island.

Ermoupolis is the main harbour on the island. The shipyard there is the largest one in Greece.

This map shows the southern half of Syros. You can see where Alkinos lives and goes to school.

Ano Syros

Monastery

Kini

Alkinos's school

ERMOUPOLIS

Marina

Lazaretta

Lighthouse

SYROS

Manna

Airport

Azolimnos

Ano Mana

Alkinos's house

Galissas

Vari

Achladi

Foinikas

Marina

Poseidonia

Agathopes

Megas Yalos

N

Komito

0   2   4 kilometres

0   2   4 miles

Lighthouse

Apart from Ermoupolis, there are only villages like Ano Mana, where Alkinos lives. Ano Mana is 5 kilometres from Ermoupolis. Only 800 people live there. There are no shops, so the villagers have to go to Ermoupolis to buy everything they need.

Landscape and Weather

Mainland Greece is made up of rocky mountains and deep, forested valleys. The landscape of Syros is similar. The mountainous centre is surrounded by a ragged coastline with bays and beaches.

Alkinos needs sunblock cream during the hot summer months.

Greece has a temperate climate, with warm, wet winters and hot, dry summers. Syros doesn't get as hot or as cold as the mainland because it is surrounded by the sea. In the summer, winds called the *meltemia* keep the island cooler than the mainland.

Greece has about 2,000 islands, of which 169 are inhabited. The islands make up about 20 per cent of the total land area.

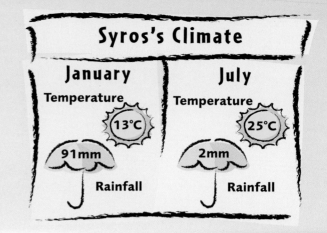

Syros's Climate

January
Temperature
13°C

91mm

Rainfall

July
Temperature
25°C

2mm

Rainfall

At Home

Alkinos lives in a house on a hillside above Ano Mana. It has eight rooms, including a bedroom each for Alkinos and Dafni. There is also an annexe for friends and family to stay when they visit from the mainland.

Alkinos's home (centre) has been built in the traditional way, with local stone.

Alkinos has lots of toy
planes and helicopters
in his bedroom.

All the rooms in the house are air-conditioned to keep
them cool in the summer. To help save water, there is a
recycling system which allows waste water to be reused.

The family play games
and watch television
in the sitting room.
There is an open fire
for burning logs in
the winter.

Outside the house there is a big garden, a terrace next to a swimming pool, and a tool shed. Olive and lemon trees grow in the garden, as they do in most Greek homes. Alkinos's mother uses the olives and lemons in her cooking.

Most Greek homes have a terrace like this one for enjoying the sunny weather.

Alkinos helps his father to put up a new shelf. Alkinos hopes he'll learn his father's skills.

Friday, 21 May

P O Box 104
Ano Mana
84–100 Syros
Greece

Yasoo Nickie!

Thanks for your letter. We've got a dog, too. She's called Edda. We've also got two rabbits, Bax and Banny. They live in a walled-off area in the garden, along with some ducks and chickens. We keep the chickens for fun and for the eggs they produce. They only lay eggs when they're in the mood! It's my job to feed them every day. We buy special food for them, as well as giving them any leftovers from our meals. I have to keep their pen clean and make sure they've always got water to drink.

From
Alkinos

Here I am topping up the food for the ducks and chickens.

Food and Mealtimes

For breakfast, Alkinos has a glass of milk with bread and jam or honey. The honey is made on the island. The bees like Syros's warm climate and sunny summers. The sun makes the plants produce a lot of nectar for the bees to collect and turn into honey.

Alkinos uses a special honey spoon that is designed for the honey to drip off easily.

Alkinos and his family have spaghetti and salad for lunch.

Lunch is often pasta with homemade beef burgers, fish or pulses, and a salad. In the evening, dinner is usually a light meal – perhaps cheese and bacon on toast and a glass of milk. Alkinos's favourite meal is a pork steak with chips and a big glass of peach juice.

Alkinos helps his mum prepare some salad for lunch by slicing up juicy, locally grown tomatoes.

Alkinos and his mum shop for fresh fruit and vegetables in Ermoupolis.

There are no shops in Ano Mano, so the family have to buy all their food in the supermarkets and street markets of Ermoupolis. It takes 10 minutes to get there by car.

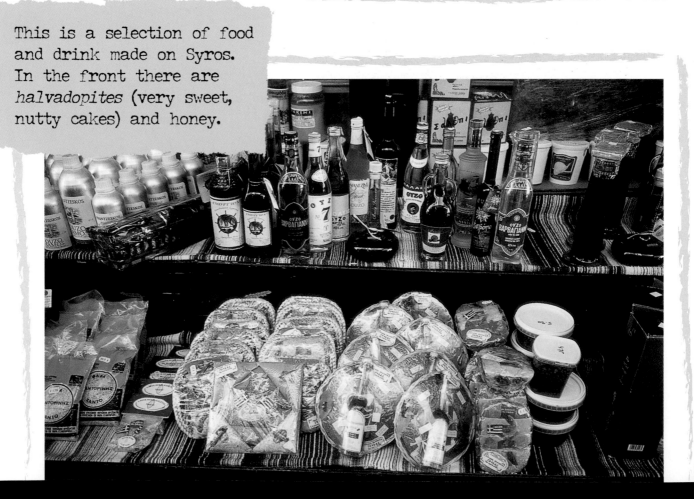

This is a selection of food and drink made on Syros. In the front there are *halvadopites* (very sweet, nutty cakes) and honey.

Sunday, 30 May

P O Box 104

Ano Mana

84–100 Syros

Greece

Hi Nickie,

Try this recipe for *takos*, which is feta and tomato bread.

You will need: 4 slices brown bread, 4 ripe tomatoes, feta cheese, fresh basil and oregano leaves, olive oil, salt and pepper.

1. Lay the bread on a dish and drizzle some oil over it.
2. Skin, de-seed and chop up the tomatoes and put them on top of the bread.
3. Crumble the cheese on to the tomatoes.
4. Cut up the herb leaves and scatter them on top, along with more oil, and salt and pepper to taste.

Kali oreksi! (Enjoy your food!)

From

Alkinos

Here I am, with a big plate of *takos*. Everyone on Syros loves *takos* – and it's good for you too!

School Day

Alkinos gets up for school at 7.30 a.m. He and Dafni catch the school bus to Ermoupolis. The bus picks up children from all over the island. Their school is called Ag Yiorgos. 'Ag' is short for Agios, the Greek word for 'saint', so in English it would be called St George's School.

Alkinos and Dafni are walking up the steps to their school.

School starts at 8.30 a.m. with assembly. There are 25 children in Alkinos's class. They study maths, modern Greek, history, geography, science and music in their lessons.

Like most schools in Greece, Ag Yiorgos is a mixed school and there is no school uniform.

In a geography lesson, the class learns about wind and how it affects sailing boats.

Alkinos usually has some homework to do every evening. Here he is doing his geography homework on Greece at his bedroom desk.

At 11 a.m. there is break, when the children go out to the playground. School ends at 2 p.m., when Alkinos and his sister get the bus home for lunch.

After school, Alkinos often goes to learn how to play tennis at a tennis club.

Tuesday, 8 June

P O Box 104
Ano Mana
84-100 Syros
Greece

Hi Nickie,

Ti kanis? (How are you?)

I'm glad you liked the *takos*. You asked what sports we do in Greece. We're lucky because the weather is good enough to spend a lot of time outdoors. At school we play a game called handball. It's a mixture of basketball and football. We're not allowed to kick the ball in the playground, so we use our hands to pass the ball and shoot at the goal.

Do you like sport? Write back and tell me!

From

Alkinos

I'm the best goalie among my friends. Nothing gets past me!

Off to Work

Alkinos's parents are interior designers. They run a small business designing the interiors of houses and offices. There are many small businesses on Syros, from farming and woodworking to hotels and cafés.

Alkinos's mum and dad discuss ideas for the design of a new house.

Traditional wooden fishing boats are still made on Syros, but most boats are now made from metal.

In Greece as a whole, 20 per cent of workers have jobs in farming, another 20 per cent work in industries and 60 per cent have jobs in services, such as banks and tourism. Millions of visitors come to Greece every year to see the islands and the remains of Ancient Greece. Greece earns a lot of money from tourism.

During the summer this ferry from Piraeus, near Athens, brings thousands of holidaymakers to Syros.

Free Time

On summer evenings and at weekends, Alkinos and his family often go to the beach at Achladi, which is about 6 kilometres away from their home (see map on page 7). After a swim, they usually have a meal at the taverna by the water's edge.

Most beaches in Greece have a taverna with seating outside so people can enjoy the view.

Alkinos and Dafnia like to play on the empty land next to their home.

There is a theatre and a cinema in Ermoupolis, which Alkinos and his family go to sometimes. But for most of his free time, Alkinos plays in Ano Mana with Dafni or his friends. They make up their own games and climb about in the trees.

When the weather's bad, Alkinos sometimes plays games on his parents' office computer.

Religion

Like most people in Greece, Alkinos and his family belong to the Greek Orthodox Church. Orthodox Christians split from Protestants and Roman Catholics hundreds of years ago. Today most Greek Orthodox people live in eastern Europe and Russia.

At this Greek Orthodox christening ceremony, the priest is about to make the sign of the cross on the baby's forehead with water from the font.

Some people in Greece are Catholic. In this Catholic church service, worshippers are receiving Communion from the priest.

Wednesday, 23 March

P O Box 104

Ano Mana

84–100 Syros

Greece

Hi Nickie,

Thanks for your letter. Your football team sounds great.

It's been really fun here this week because it's been *Apokries*. I think you would call this Carnival. *Apokries* is a noisy, lively festival held in March or April, when we celebrate the end of winter and prepare for Lent. There's a lot of singing and dancing, street parades and fancy-dress parties. It's great fun. When it's over, everyone quietens down for Lent.

From

Alkinos

Here I am with Dafni, dressed up for *Apokries*. Who do you think looks more scary?

Fact File

Capital city: Athens. People come here to see the famous Acropolis, the buildings on the hillside on the right.

Other major cities: Thessaloniki, Volos, Piraeus, Patrai.

Neighbouring countries: Albania, Bulgaria, Macedonia, Turkey.

Size: 131,940km².

Population: 10,647,529.

Languages: Greek, English, French.

Main industries: Tourism, food and tobacco processing, textiles, chemicals, metal products.

Flag: Horizontal strips of blue and white, with a white cross on a blue square in the top left corner. The cross stands for the Greek Orthodox religion.

Currency: The euro, divided into cents (1 euro=100 cents).

Main religions: About 98 per cent of the population are Greek Orthodox and 1.3 per cent are Muslim. The rest are mainly Christian Roman Catholics.

Olympic Games: The first Olympic Games were held in Greece in 776 BC. They were last held in Greece in 2004. The Olympic flame always burns during the Games. It can be seen below on the right.

History: About 4,000 years ago the Ancient Greeks created the first civilization in Europe. It was very advanced and powerful. They were conquered first by the Romans and then by the Turks. In 1829, Greece became independent. It is now part of the European Union.

Highest point: Mount Olympus (2,917m).

Longest river: Aliákmonas (314km).

Main festivals: Independence Day (25 March), when Greeks celebrate freedom from Turkish rule, *Apokries* (Carnival) and Easter.

Famous Greeks: Alexander the Great (356–323 BC) had an empire stretching from Greece to India. Prince Philip, husband of Queen Elizabeth II of Britain, was born on the island of Corfu and is the son of a Greek prince.

Stamps: Greek stamps show all sorts of things, including the army and navy, religion and the Olympic Games.

Glossary

air-conditioned Somewhere that has the air temperature controlled by a machine.

Ancient Greeks People who lived in Greece from earliest times until about 400 BC.

capital The most important town or city in a country.

civilization A people with a well-organized country.

Communion The Christian ceremony in which holy bread and wine are given to worshippers by a priest.

feta cheese A Greek cheese made from sheep or goats' milk.

harbour A place where ships can load and unload.

inhabited Lived in.

mainland Greece The main part of Greece, not the islands around it.

philosophy The study of the principles of human behaviour and how the universe works.

population All the people who live in one place, like a country or a city.

shipyard A large yard where ships are built or repaired.

sunblock A substance that stops the sun's harmful rays from damaging skin.

taverna A Greek café or restaurant.

temperate Neither extremely hot nor extremely cold.

tourism The business connected with tourists, people who visit other countries for pleasure.

Further Information

Information books:

Ancient Olympics by Shahrukh Husain (Evans, 2003)

Changing Face of Greece by Tamsin Osler (Hodder Wayland, 2003)

Horrible Histories: The Groovy Greeks by Terry Deary (Scholastic Hippo, 2004

Illustrated Guide to Greek Myths and Legends by C. Evans (Usborne, 2004)

A World of Recipes: Greece by Sue Townsend (Heinemann, 2003)

Fiction:

Atticus the Storyteller's 100 Greek Myths by Lucy Coats (Orion, 2003)

Stories from Ancient Greece by Shahrukh Husain (Evans, 2003)

Resource packs:

Spend the Day in Ancient Greece: Projects and Activities that Bring the Past to Life by Lesley Miles (Usborne, 2004)

Websites:

CIA World Factbook
www.cia.gov/cia/publications/
factbook/
Facts and figures about Greece and other countries.

Athens 2004
www.athens2004.com/
Everything you want to know about the most recent Olympic Games.

BBC Schools
www.bbc.co.uk/schools/
Useful curriculum-based information plus links to schools TV and radio.

Best of History
www.besthistorysites.net/
The Ancient Greece site is packed with detailed facts and many links.

Index